Psychic Your Pocket

Paula Wratten

© paula wratten

Paula Wratten - Author, Body Holography Interpreter, Quantum Healing Practitioner & Teacher, Light Language Therapist, Intuitive Healer.

Paula Wratten is a multi-talented individual with a passion for healing, transformation, and spiritual exploration. As an accomplished author, she has written two insightful books that delve into the depths of consciousness, personal growth, and holistic well-being.

Copyright Paula Wratten ©

The material contained within this article must not be shared or distributed without the permission of the writer. Please respect the privacy of the recipient, all information is confidential. Intellectual rights apply.

Thank you to my husband for putting up with my crazy ideas, late nights and constant questions about technical stuff x

Introduction

Life is a journey filled with twists and turns, highs and lows, moments of clarity, and times of confusion. At every step, we are faced with decisions and challenges that shape our path. While it may seem that we are navigating this journey alone, we possess a powerful tool that can guide us through even the most difficult times: our inner psychic.

The concept of having a "psychic in your pocket" is about tapping into your innate wisdom and intuition. It's about learning to trust yourself, to listen to that quiet inner voice that often knows the right path, even when our logical mind is uncertain. This book is designed to help you develop and harness this inner psychic to navigate life's problems with confidence and grace.

Everyone has an inner psychic, an intuitive part of themselves that can sense the best course of action.

This isn't about predicting the future in a supernatural sense, but rather about becoming attuned to your inner guidance system. Your intuition is like a compass, providing subtle nudges and insights that can lead you toward your true purpose and away from unnecessary struggles.

Developing your inner psychic is a practice that requires time and effort. This book will include a variety of exercises and meditations designed to strengthen your intuition and connect you with your inner wisdom. These practical tools will help you integrate the concepts discussed throughout the book into your daily life.

Quote:

"Life's true healing begins when we embrace each scar as a chapter of our story, for within the cracks of our brokenness lies the light of our resilience." Paula Wratten

Chapter Title 1

Understanding your inner psychic involves recognising and cultivating the intuitive abilities that reside within each of us. This inner psychic is not about possessing supernatural powers, but about being attuned to your inner voice and gut feelings that often guide you toward the best decisions.

It means developing a keen sense of self-awareness and trust in your instincts, which can provide clarity and direction in times of uncertainty. By tuning into this inner wisdom, you can navigate life's challenges more effectively, recognising subtle signals and insights that help you make choices aligned with your true self.

Embracing your inner psychic empowers you to live a more authentic and fulfilled life, as you learn to rely on your inherent guidance system to steer you through the complexities of daily living.

Accessing Your Inner Psychic: Unlocking the Wisdom Within

In the hustle and bustle of modern life, it's easy to overlook the quiet, guiding voice of our inner psychic. This inner wisdom, often referred to as intuition, is an inherent part of each of us, offering insights and guidance when we most need it. Accessing your inner psychic doesn't require supernatural abilities; it involves honing a few simple practices to connect with your intuitive self.

Here's how you can start:

1. Cultivate Mindfulness

Mindfulness is the foundation for accessing your inner psychic. By being present and fully engaged in the moment, you can quiet the noise of daily life and tune into your inner thoughts and feelings. Practices like meditation, deep breathing, and mindful observation help you become more aware of subtle cues and insights that your intuition provides.

2. Listen to Your Gut Feelings

Your gut feelings are powerful indicators of your inner psychic. These instincts are often your subconscious mind's way of processing information and guiding you toward the best decision. When you experience a strong gut feeling, take a moment to pause and reflect on it. Trusting these feelings can lead you to make more aligned choices.

3. Keep a Journal

Journaling is an excellent way to access and understand your inner psychic. By regularly writing down your thoughts, dreams, and feelings, you create a space to explore your inner world. Over time, patterns and insights will emerge, helping you recognise the voice of your intuition. Reviewing your journal can also provide clarity on past decisions and guide future ones.

4. Practice Visualisation

Visualisation exercises can help you tap into your inner psychic. Spend a few minutes each day imagining a situation or decision you are facing. Visualise different outcomes and pay attention to how each one feels. This practice can reveal intuitive preferences and insights that might not be immediately obvious through logical thinking alone.

5. Pay Attention to Synchronicities

Synchronicities are meaningful coincidences that can serve as messages from your inner psychic. When you notice patterns or unusual coincidences in your life, take note of them. These events can provide valuable guidance and affirm that you are on the right path. Trust that these synchronicities are not mere chance, but rather signs that your intuition is at work.

6. Create a Quiet Space

Having a dedicated space for quiet reflection can enhance your connection to your inner psychic. This space doesn't have to be elaborate; it can be a corner of a room where you feel comfortable and at peace. Regularly spending time in this space, free from distractions, allows you to tune into your inner wisdom more effectively.

7. Trust Yourself

The most crucial step in accessing your inner psychic is learning to trust yourself. Doubt and fear can cloud your intuition, making it difficult to hear your inner voice. Affirmations and positive self-talk can reinforce your belief in your own abilities. Remind yourself that your intuition is a natural and reliable part of who you are.

By incorporating these practices into your daily routine, you can strengthen your connection to your inner psychic and navigate life's challenges with greater confidence and clarity. Remember, your intuition is always there, ready to guide you; all you need to do is listen.

"When you doubt your intuition, remember that it is the voice of your soul whispering truths that your mind has yet to understand. Trust in the quiet knowing within, for it is connected to the infinite wisdom of the universe. In the stillness of your heart, you will find the guidance you seek."

Chapter 2
Overcoming Fear and Doubt: Embracing Your Inner Strength

Fear and doubt are natural emotions that everyone experiences, but they can become significant obstacles on the path to personal growth and fulfilment. Overcoming these feelings is crucial for accessing your inner wisdom and living a life aligned with your true purpose. Here are some strategies to help you conquer fear and doubt and embrace your inner strength:

1. Acknowledge Your Fears

The first step in overcoming fear is to acknowledge it. Denying or ignoring your fears only gives them more power. Take a moment to identify what exactly you are afraid of. Is it failure, rejection, the unknown? By naming your fears, you can begin to address them directly.

2. Challenge Negative Thoughts

Fear and doubt often stem from negative thoughts and beliefs about ourselves. Challenge these thoughts by asking whether they are based on facts or assumptions. Replace negative self-talk with positive affirmations. Remind yourself of past successes and times when you overcame challenges.

3. Take Small Steps

Overcoming fear doesn't mean you have to take giant leaps. Start with small, manageable steps that move you out of your comfort zone. Each small success builds confidence and reduces the power of fear. Celebrate your progress, no matter how small it may seem.

4. Visualise Success

Visualisation is a powerful tool for overcoming fear and doubt. Spend a few minutes each day imagining yourself succeeding in the areas where you feel fear. Picture yourself confidently navigating challenges and achieving your goals. Visualisation can help rewire your brain to expect positive outcomes.

5. Practice Mindfulness and Meditation

Mindfulness and meditation can help calm the mind and reduce anxiety. By focusing on the present moment, you can prevent fear and doubt from overwhelming you. Regular meditation practice can increase your resilience and improve your ability to cope with stress.

6. Seek Support

You don't have to face your fears alone. Reach out to friends, family, or a mentor for support and encouragement. Sometimes, just talking about your fears can lessen their hold on you. Support groups or therapy can also provide valuable tools and perspectives for overcoming fear and doubt.

7. Embrace Failure as a Learning Opportunity

Fear of failure is a common obstacle, but failure is often a necessary step toward success. Reframe failure as a learning opportunity rather than a setback. Each failure provides valuable lessons and insights that can help you grow and improve.

8. Stay Grounded in Your Purpose

When fear and doubt arise, reconnect with your deeper purpose and values. Remind yourself why you are pursuing your goals and what you hope to achieve. Staying grounded in your purpose can provide the motivation and courage needed to push through fear.

9. Cultivate Resilience

Resilience is the ability to bounce back from adversity. Strengthening your resilience can help you face fear and doubt with greater confidence. Practices such as maintaining a positive attitude, staying flexible, and developing problem-solving skills can enhance your resilience.

10. Trust Yourself

Ultimately, overcoming fear and doubt requires trusting yourself and your abilities. Believe that you have the strength and resources to handle whatever comes your way. Trusting yourself doesn't mean you will never feel fear or doubt, but it does mean you won't let these feelings control you.

By implementing these strategies, you can begin to overcome fear and doubt, opening the door to a more confident and fulfilling life. Remember, courage is not the absence of fear, but the willingness to move forward despite it. Embrace your inner strength, and trust that you have the power to navigate any challenge that comes your way.

"Fear is the shadow that dims the light of your true potential. Embrace it, understand it, and let it guide you to the edges of your comfort zone, for it is there that your inner strength resides. Trust in the boundless power of your spirit, and know that within you lies the courage to overcome any challenge. When you face fear with an open heart, you transform it into a stepping stone towards your greatest self."

Chapter 3

Finding Your True Purpose: A Journey to Fulfilment

In the quest for a meaningful and fulfilling life, finding your true purpose stands as a central goal. This sense of purpose gives direction, motivation, and a deeper sense of satisfaction. Yet, discovering what truly drives and fulfils you can be a daunting task. Here are some steps and reflections to help you uncover your true purpose.

1. Self-Reflection: The First Step

The journey to finding your true purpose begins with self-reflection. Take time to look inward and ask yourself fundamental questions: What are my passions? What activities make me lose track of time? What values are most important to me? Journaling your thoughts and feelings can help clarify what resonates most deeply with you.

2. Identify Your Strengths and Talents

Everyone has unique strengths and talents. Recognising what you excel at can provide valuable clues to your purpose. Think about the skills you've developed over time, the compliments you frequently receive, and the tasks you find easiest to perform. These strengths can point you toward areas where you can make a meaningful impact.

3. Listen to Your Inner Voice

Your inner voice, or intuition, can be a powerful guide in finding your true purpose. This inner guidance often whispers to you through feelings, hunches, or persistent thoughts. Pay attention to what your intuition is telling you about your path and be open to the subtle nudges that steer you in the right direction.

4. Explore Your Interests

Exploring different interests can help you uncover hidden passions. Try new activities, volunteer, take classes, and expose yourself to various fields. You might discover an unexpected interest that sparks a sense of purpose. Don't be afraid to step out of your comfort zone and experiment.

5. Consider Your Impact on Others

Purpose often lies in how we contribute to the well-being of others. Reflect on how you can make a positive difference in the lives of those around you. Whether through your career, hobbies, or personal relationships, consider ways in which your actions can benefit others and bring you fulfilment.

6. Align with Your Values

Your core values are the principles that guide your decisions and behaviour. Identifying and aligning with these values is crucial for finding your true purpose. Make a list of your top values and evaluate how well your current lifestyle aligns with them. Living in accordance with your values will bring a greater sense of purpose and integrity.

7. Seek Inspiration from Others

Look to role models and mentors who inspire you. Learn about their journeys and how they discovered their purpose. Engaging with a community of like-minded individuals can provide support, motivation, and new perspectives. Surround yourself with people who encourage and uplift you.

8. Be Patient and Persistent

Finding your true purpose is a journey that takes time and patience. It's okay if you don't have all the answers right away. Stay persistent in your search and remain open to change. As you grow and evolve, your understanding of your purpose may also shift.

9. Embrace Challenges and Setbacks

Challenges and setbacks are a natural part of any journey. Instead of seeing them as failures, view them as opportunities for growth and learning. Overcoming obstacles can provide valuable insights and bring you closer to understanding your true purpose.

10. Trust the Process

Finally, trust that you are on the right path, even if it's not always clear. Have faith in your journey and trust that each step, no matter how small, is leading you toward your true purpose. Let go of the need for immediate answers and allow your purpose to unfold naturally.

Conclusion

Finding your true purpose is a deeply personal and transformative journey. It involves self-discovery, introspection, and a willingness to embrace change. By reflecting on your passions, strengths, values, and the impact you wish to make, you can uncover a sense of purpose that brings meaning and fulfilment to your life. Remember, your purpose is not a destination but an ongoing journey of growth and self-realisation. Trust in yourself and the process, and you will find the path that resonates with your true essence.

"Finding your true purpose is a sacred journey that aligns your soul with the universe's grand design. Trust that within you lies a unique light, a divine spark waiting to illuminate your path. Embrace each moment with an open heart and a curious spirit, for every experience and challenge is a step toward revealing your higher calling. Listen to the whispers of your intuition, honor your passions, and let your values guide you. As you walk this path, remember that you are never alone; the universe supports and guides you, leading you to a life of profound meaning and boundless joy. Your true purpose is not just a destination, but a beautiful unfolding of your authentic self."

Chapter 4

Embracing Change: A Spiritual Journey of Transformation

Change is an inevitable part of life's journey, a constant force that shapes our experiences and shapes who we become. Yet, embracing change is often met with resistance and fear. In this book, we explore the spiritual dimensions of embracing change as a profound opportunity for growth, transformation, and alignment with our higher selves.

1. Understanding the Nature of Change

Change is not merely external circumstances shifting; it is a spiritual invitation to evolve and expand our consciousness. Just as seasons change and cycles renew, so too do our lives ebb and flow with change. Recognising this natural rhythm allows us to embrace change with grace and acceptance.

2. Surrendering to the Flow

Spiritual teachings often emphasise the importance of surrendering to the flow of life. Embracing change involves letting go of resistance and trusting in the divine order of the universe. It requires releasing attachments to outcomes and embracing the present moment with gratitude and mindfulness.

3. Cultivating Inner Resilience

Change can challenge our sense of stability and security, but it also offers an opportunity to cultivate inner resilience. Spiritual practices such as meditation, prayer, and mindfulness can strengthen our inner core, enabling us to navigate uncertainty with courage and grace.

4. Finding Meaning and Purpose

Every change, no matter how challenging, holds within it the seeds of growth and transformation. By embracing change, we open ourselves to new opportunities and possibilities aligned with our true purpose. Spiritual exploration helps us uncover deeper meanings and insights that guide us on our path.

5. Honouring Transitions and Cycles

In spiritual traditions worldwide, rituals and ceremonies mark significant life transitions. Embracing change involves honoring these transitions as sacred rites of passage, acknowledging the wisdom and lessons they bring. By embracing rituals that align with our spiritual beliefs, we can navigate change with reverence and intention.

6. Trusting in Divine Timing

Trust is a cornerstone of spiritual growth, especially when facing uncertainty and change. Trusting in divine timing means surrendering our need for control and believing that everything unfolds according to a higher plan. This trust allows us to approach change with faith and patience, knowing that we are supported by a loving and benevolent universe.

7. Embracing Impermanence

Spiritual teachings often remind us of the impermanent nature of all things. Embracing change involves embracing impermanence as a fundamental aspect of life. By accepting that nothing lasts forever, we can appreciate each moment and experience fully, without clinging to the past or fearing the future.

8. Connecting with Universal Oneness

Change can create a sense of separation and disconnection, yet it also offers an opportunity to deepen our connection with universal oneness. Spiritual practices such as compassion, forgiveness, and gratitude foster a sense of interconnectedness with all beings and the universe itself. Embracing change becomes a spiritual practice that aligns us with the flow of life and the interconnected web of existence.

Conclusion

Embracing change is not about avoiding discomfort or uncertainty, but about embracing the inherent wisdom and transformative power it offers. By integrating spiritual principles into our approach to change, we can navigate life's transitions with greater ease, resilience, and grace.

This book invites you to embark on a spiritual journey of embracing change as a profound opportunity for growth, transformation, and alignment with your higher self. Through spiritual wisdom and practices, you can learn to embrace change as a sacred gift on your path to personal and spiritual fulfilment.

"Embracing change is not just about adapting to new circumstances; it's about evolving into the person you are destined to become, guided by the wisdom gained from each transformative moment."

Chapter 5

Achieving Balance And Harmony

Achieving balance and harmony is about aligning your inner self with the outer world, finding equilibrium amidst life's diverse demands. It requires a mindful blend of self-awareness, prioritisation, and conscious choices that nurture both your personal well-being and your responsibilities.

By honouring your physical, mental, emotional, and spiritual needs while maintaining healthy boundaries, you cultivate a sense of inner peace and fulfilment. Striving for balance is not about perfection but about continuous adjustment and alignment, fostering resilience and harmony in every facet of life.

Finding and achieving balance and harmony in life is a journey that requires conscious effort and self-awareness. Here are some practical steps to help you in this pursuit:

1. Self-Reflection and Assessment

- Evaluate Your Current Situation: Take time to assess how balanced your life currently feels. Identify areas where you may have overextended yourself or neglected important aspects such as health, relationships, work, and personal growth.

- Reflect on Your Values: Clarify your core values and priorities. Understanding what matters most to you will guide your decisions and help you allocate time and energy accordingly.

2. Set Clear Priorities and Boundaries

- Define Your Goals: Establish clear goals for different areas of your life, such as health, career, relationships, and personal development. Setting priorities allows you to focus on what is most important to you.

- Learn to Say No: Setting boundaries is crucial for maintaining balance. Practice saying no to commitments or activities that do not align with your priorities or values, to avoid overcommitment and burnout.

3. Create a Balanced Routine

- Schedule Regular Self-Care: Make time for activities that nourish your physical, mental, and emotional well-being, such as exercise, meditation, hobbies, and relaxation.

- Manage Your Time Wisely: Organise your schedule to include time for work, relationships, personal interests, and rest. Use tools like calendars or planners to structure your day effectively.

4. Nurture Healthy Relationships

- Cultivate Supportive Connections: Surround yourself with people who uplift and support you. Nurture relationships that bring positivity and fulfilment into your life.

- Communicate Effectively: Open communication is essential for maintaining harmonious relationships. Practice active listening and express your needs and feelings openly and respectfully.

5. Practice Mindfulness and Stress Management

- Mindfulness Meditation: Engage in mindfulness practices to stay present and reduce stress. Mindfulness helps you appreciate each moment and respond to challenges with clarity and composure.

- Stress Reduction Techniques: Incorporate relaxation techniques such as deep breathing, yoga, or nature walks to manage stress and promote inner peace.

6. Embrace Flexibility and Adaptability

- Accept Imperfection: Understand that achieving balance is a continuous process and perfection is unrealistic. Embrace flexibility and adjust your approach as needed to maintain equilibrium in changing circumstances.

- Learn from Challenges: View setbacks as opportunities for growth and learning. Resilience in the face of adversity contributes to long-term balance and harmony.

7. Seek Professional Support if Needed

- Therapy or Counselling: Consider seeking professional help if you struggle with maintaining balance or managing stress effectively. A therapist can provide guidance and support tailored to your specific needs.

8. Celebrate Progress and Practice Gratitude

- Acknowledge Your Achievements: Celebrate small victories and milestones along your journey towards balance and harmony. Recognising your progress boosts motivation and reinforces positive habits.

- Gratitude Practice: Cultivate gratitude for the blessings in your life, both big and small. Gratitude fosters contentment and helps you focus on the positive aspects of your journey.

Conclusion

Achieving balance and harmony is a dynamic process that requires self-awareness, intentional choices, and continuous adjustment.

By prioritising your well-being, setting clear boundaries, nurturing relationships, practicing mindfulness, and embracing flexibility, you can create a life that feels aligned with your values and brings you a sense of peace and fulfilment. Remember, balance is not a destination but a journey of self-discovery and growth.

"Balance and harmony are the art of living consciously and gracefully amidst the ebb and flow of life's challenges and joys. Like a skilled tightrope walker, we navigate between our ambitions and our serenity, ensuring that neither overwhelms the other. It's about finding equilibrium between work and rest, ambition and contentment, solitude and connection. In this delicate dance, we honour our values and priorities, nurturing our physical, emotional, and spiritual well-being with mindful intention. When we achieve balance and harmony, we create a symphony of existence where each note, though distinct, blends seamlessly into the melody of a fulfilling life."

Chapter 6

Practical Exercises:

Journaling Intuition:

> Keep a journal dedicated to recording your intuitive insights, dreams, and hunches. Review your entries regularly to track patterns and strengthen your connection to your inner guidance.

Daily Intuitive Practice:

- Practice intuitive exercises daily, such as guessing who is calling before answering the phone, sensing the energy of a room upon entering, or intuitively selecting a book or movie without overthinking.

Enhance Sensory Awareness:

- Engage in activities that heighten your senses, such as mindful eating (noticing flavours and textures), listening to nature sounds, or practicing tactile awareness (feeling textures and temperatures).

Developing Clairvoyance:

- Use visualisation exercises to imagine specific scenarios or objects in detail. Practice seeing colours, shapes, and symbols with your mind's eye, gradually expanding your ability to visualise.

Psychometry Practice:

- Practice psychometry by holding an object (such as a piece of jewellery or a photograph) and focusing on any impressions or sensations that come to you. Trust your initial instincts and jot down your impressions.

Meditations:

Guided Visualisation:

- Use guided meditations focused on enhancing psychic abilities. Visualise yourself surrounded by a protective light, then explore your intuitive senses, such as seeing images or sensing emotions.

Chakra Meditation:

- Focus on balancing and aligning your chakras through meditation. Start from the root chakra and work your way up to the crown chakra, visualising each chakra as a spinning wheel of energy emitting vibrant colours.

Third Eye Activation:

- Meditate specifically on awakening and activating your third eye chakra (located between your eyebrows). Imagine a bright indigo light expanding from this point, opening your intuition and inner sight.

Breathing Exercises:

- Practice deep breathing exercises to calm the mind and enhance your receptivity to psychic impressions. Inhale deeply through the nose, hold for a count, and exhale slowly through the mouth, releasing tension.

Connecting with Spirit Guides:

- Meditate to establish or strengthen connections with your spirit guides or higher self. Set the intention to receive guidance and wisdom, and be open to subtle messages, feelings, or images that arise during meditation.

Tips for Practicing:

- Consistency: Regular practice is key to developing psychic abilities. Dedicate time each day or week to exercises and meditations that resonate with you.

- Trust Your Intuition: Trust your initial impressions and intuitive insights, even if they seem subtle or unclear at first. Practice acknowledging and validating your intuitive experiences.

- Create a Sacred Space: Establish a quiet and comfortable space for your psychic exercises and meditations. Use candles, crystals, or calming music to enhance your practice environment.

- Stay Grounded: After psychic exercises or meditations, ground yourself by connecting with nature, walking barefoot on the earth, or enjoying a grounding meal.

By integrating these practical exercises and meditations into your routine, you can cultivate and strengthen your psychic abilities over time, fostering a deeper connection to your intuition and spiritual awareness.

"Trust the process unfolding before you, for it is intricately woven with the threads of your journey. Like a tapestry being crafted with care and purpose, each moment holds meaning and lessons that shape your path. Embrace the uncertainties with faith, knowing that every twist and turn is guiding you towards growth and alignment with your highest good. Trust in the wisdom of divine timing, and allow patience to nurture the seeds of your dreams. As you surrender to the flow of life, you align with the universe's intricate design, where trust becomes the bridge that connects you to the infinite possibilities of your soul's journey."

Chapter 7

In conclusion, trusting your journey is about embracing the unfolding of life with faith and surrender. It requires a deep belief in your inner wisdom and the divine timing that orchestrates each step of your path. By cultivating patience and resilience, you allow yourself to navigate challenges with grace, knowing that every experience, whether joyful or difficult, serves a purpose in your growth. Trusting your journey means honouring your intuition, staying true to your values, and embracing the unknown with an open heart. As you continue forward, remember that your journey is uniquely yours, filled with opportunities for learning, healing, and profound transformation. Trust in the process, for it leads you towards a life of fulfilment, authenticity, and alignment with your highest self.

Chapter 8

When Life gives you lemons! An alternative look at life.

"When life gives you lemons, it's not just about making lemonade; it's an invitation to embrace the essence of transformation. Lemons, with their tangy zest and vibrant colour, symbolise the unexpected challenges and sour moments that life inevitably presents. In these moments, we're reminded that adversity is not merely a setback but a catalyst for growth and resilience.

Just as lemonade transforms the tartness of lemons into a refreshing drink, so too, can we transform adversity into opportunities for learning and personal evolution. The process involves squeezing out the lessons hidden within challenges, extracting wisdom, and infusing it into the fabric of our lives. It's about turning bitterness into sweetness, finding gratitude in difficulty, and discovering strength in vulnerability.

Moreover, when life gives you lemons, it encourages a shift in perspective—a reminder to embrace change with creativity and optimism. It challenges us to innovate, to explore new flavours of experience, and to savour the unique opportunities that come with overcoming obstacles.

Ultimately, embracing life's lemons is about harnessing their potential to enrich our journey, deepen our resilience, and cultivate a zest for life that transcends the sour moments."

Chapter 9

A unique perspective on the saying "when it rains it pours:"

"When it rains, it pours—a familiar adage that speaks not just of challenges and difficulties, but of the profound transformations that accompany them. Imagine the rain not as a deluge of troubles, but as a cleansing shower washing away the old, nourishing the earth, and preparing the ground for new growth.

In life, moments of intensity often coincide, overwhelming us with a cascade of events and emotions. Yet, within this downpour lies an opportunity for renewal and rebirth. Like seeds buried beneath the soil, adversity provides fertile ground for resilience to take root and for wisdom to blossom.

When it rains, it pours, beckoning us to look beyond the immediate discomfort and see the potential for growth and renewal. It urges us to trust in the natural cycles of life—to embrace the storm with courage, knowing that it will pass, leaving us stronger, wiser, and more attuned to the rhythms of our journey.

So, when life's challenges converge like a torrential rain, remember that within the chaos lies the promise of transformation. Embrace the downpour, for it is in the midst of storms that we often find the clarity, strength, and resilience to weather any tempest that comes our way."

Chapter 10

Every Cloud Has A Silver Lining, Seeing things from a different perspective

"Every cloud has a silver lining is not just a saying, but a timeless reminder that even amidst life's darkest moments, there exists a glimmer of hope and opportunity. Picture a stormy sky where clouds gather, casting shadows over the landscape. In these moments, it's easy to feel overwhelmed by the gloom and uncertainty.

Yet, if we shift our perspective, we can see that within every cloud, there is a silver lining waiting to be discovered. It's a reminder to look beyond the surface and find the hidden blessings, lessons, and growth that often accompany adversity.

When challenges arise, they offer a chance for introspection and personal development. They prompt us to reassess our priorities, strengthen our resilience, and cultivate gratitude for the small victories amidst the struggle.

Moreover, the silver lining in every cloud invites us to trust in the natural unfolding of life's journey. It encourages us to believe that setbacks are temporary, and that every experience—whether joyous or challenging—contributes to our growth and evolution.

So, embrace the wisdom of 'every cloud has a silver lining' as a beacon of hope and resilience. Let it inspire you to find beauty in unexpected places, to seek lessons in adversity, and to trust that even in the darkest of times, there is always a glimmer of light waiting to guide you forward."

Chapter 11

Changing how we see the world

Trouble Comes In Threes

"Trouble comes in threes" is a belief that often surfaces during challenging times, suggesting a pattern or sequence of difficulties. Yet, what if we reframed this perspective to see it as an opportunity for growth and transformation?

Consider this: like the three acts of a story or the three stages of alchemy, challenges that come in threes may signify a complete cycle of transformation. The first trouble may shake us from our comfort zone, prompting us to reassess our situation and make necessary adjustments. The second challenge tests our resilience and determination, pushing us to dig deeper within ourselves for strength and wisdom. By the time the third trouble arrives, we have already gained valuable insights and experiences from navigating the previous challenges. We may find ourselves more equipped to face adversity with grace, clarity, and resilience.

Furthermore, the concept of "trouble comes in threes" can also be a reminder of the interconnectedness of our experiences. Just as challenges may arrive in clusters, so too can moments of growth, opportunity, and breakthroughs. Each trouble guides us towards greater self-awareness, personal development, and alignment with our true purpose as we journey forward.

Therefore, instead of dreading the arrival of the third trouble, embrace it as a catalyst for transformation. See it as an opportunity to harness the lessons learned, deepen your resilience, and emerge stronger and more empowered than before. In this way, the cycle of troubles in threes becomes a pathway to personal growth, inner strength, and profound spiritual evolution.

Chapter 12

Be twice as productive with half the effort

"Be twice as productive with half the effort" challenges conventional wisdom about hard work by advocating for smart work, emphasising efficiency, and leveraging the power of focused intention. Imagine productivity not as a measure of how much you do, but how effectively you allocate your energy and time to achieve meaningful results.

Consider the principle of a minimal effective dose: the smallest amount of effort needed to produce the desired outcome. This principle, rooted in both science and ancient wisdom, suggests that by identifying and prioritising key tasks, you can achieve maximum impact with minimal effort. It's about honing in on what truly matters and eliminating unnecessary distractions.

Additionally, this perspective invites you to harness the power of flow, a state of heightened focus and immersion where productivity naturally increases. When you align your work with your passions and strengths, you enter a state where effort feels effortless and you amplify your results.

Moreover, integrating mindfulness and intentionality into your daily routine can transform your approach to productivity. Techniques such as time blocking, prioritising high-energy periods for demanding tasks, and taking regular breaks to recharge can enhance efficiency and output.

In essence, being twice as productive with half the effort is about optimising your approach to work. It's a call to work smarter, not harder, and to align your efforts with your true purpose and strengths. By doing so, you create a balanced, fulfilling, and highly effective way of living and working, where less truly becomes more.

In this chapter we will be looking at different attitudes towards bad luck, negative energy.

Chapter 13

From a psychic perspective, people often view "bad luck" as more than just a series of unfortunate events. From a psychic perspective, one can interpret "bad luck" as a manifestation of energy imbalances, negative thought patterns, or unresolved karmic issues. Here's how to view bad luck through a psychic lens and steps to transform it into positive energy and opportunities.

Understanding Bad Luck

Energy Imbalances:

- Every person emits and attracts energy. Bad luck can sometimes be the result of negative energy accumulations in our aura or environment. This negative energy can stem from unresolved emotions, stress, or being in toxic environments.

Thought Patterns:

- Our thoughts and beliefs shape our reality. Persistent negative thinking can create a self-fulfilling prophecy where we attract more negativity into our lives. It's essential to recognise these patterns and understand how they influence our experiences.

Karmic Influences:

- Karma, the principle of cause and effect, suggests that our past actions influence our present circumstances. What might seem like bad luck could be karmic lessons that we need to learn and resolve in this lifetime.

Changing Your Luck

Cleansing and Balancing Energy:

- Smudging: Use sage, palo santo, or other cleansing herbs to clear negative energy from your space and aura. Visualise the smoke, removing negativity and restoring balance.

- Salt Baths: Regularly take baths with sea salt or Epsom salt to cleanse your energy field. Salt has natural purifying properties that help remove negative energy.

Positive Affirmations and Visualisation:

- Replace negative thought patterns with positive affirmations. Affirmations such as "I attract positive energy and opportunities" can help reprogram your mind to focus on the positive.

- Visualise yourself surrounded by a protective light, attracting positive experiences and repelling negativity.

- This practice can shift your energetic vibration and attract better outcomes.

Gratitude Practice:

- Cultivate gratitude by focusing on the positive aspects of your life. Gratitude raises your vibration and attracts more positive experiences. Keep a gratitude journal to regularly reflect on your blessings.

Karmic Healing:

- Engage in practices that help resolve karmic debts, such as forgiveness, compassion, and acts of kindness. Meditation and prayer can also facilitate karmic healing and balance.

Seek Guidance from Spirit Guides:

- Connect with your spirit guides or higher self through meditation or prayer. Ask for guidance on how to navigate through periods of bad luck and seek insights on any lessons you need to learn.

Mindfulness and Presence:

- Practice mindfulness to stay present and be aware of your thoughts and actions. Being mindful helps you make conscious choices that align with positive outcomes and reduces the impact of negative patterns.

Final Thoughts

Bad luck is not a permanent state, but a signal for change and growth. By shifting your perspective, cleansing your energy, and adopting positive practices, you can transform bad luck into opportunities for personal and spiritual development. Trust that you have the power to change your luck and attract the positive experiences you desire. Embrace these practices with faith and intention, and watch how your reality transforms for the better.

Chapter 14

Psychic Protection

However, shielding from negative energy isn't solely confined to the realm of thought; it extends into the realm of action. Deed-based shielding involves consciously engaging in practices that reinforce positivity and repel negativity from our immediate environment.

Acts of kindness, compassion, and gratitude serve as potent shields against negativity. Engaging in selfless deeds and radiating positivity through our actions generates a ripple effect, creating an aura of positivity that shields us and those around us from negative energies.

Setting boundaries and practicing self-care are integral components of deed-based shielding. Establishing healthy boundaries protects our energy by discerning what serves our well-being and what doesn't, thereby minimising exposure to draining or negative influences.

Cleansing rituals, such as smudging with sage or using crystals, offer tangible methods to purify and protect one's surroundings from negative energies. These practices, deeply rooted in various cultures and traditions, effectively dispel stagnant or harmful energies, creating a harmonious and protected space.

Psychic attacks are energetic assaults that can affect individuals on a mental, emotional, or spiritual level, often originating from negative intentions or energy sent by others. These attacks can manifest in various forms, including curses, energy vampirism, and psychic manipulation. Symptoms of psychic attacks may include sudden fatigue, unexplained physical ailments, or emotional disturbances.

Understanding psychic attacks involves recognising their signs and symptoms, differentiating them from other energetic influences, and implementing techniques for protection and healing.

Establishing and maintaining energetic boundaries is crucial in safeguarding oneself against psychic attacks, along with utilising visualisation, energy shielding, and spiritual practices for protection. Clearing and cleansing practices can also help remove negative influences from one's energy field and living spaces.

By learning to recognise, protect against, and heal from psychic attacks, individuals can reclaim their power and cultivate a greater sense of empowerment and well-being in their lives.

In conclusion, shielding oneself from negative energy, whether through thought or deed, is a multi-faceted practice that harmonises the power of mind, spirit, and action. It's a conscious endeavour that cultivates an inner sanctuary of positivity while fortifying our energetic boundaries against external negativity. By embracing these practices, individuals embark on a transformative journey towards holistic well-being, fostering resilience and inner peace amidst life's fluctuations.

Chapter 15

Dealing With False Light

False light entities are spiritual entities or energies that present themselves as benevolent, loving, or enlightened, but in reality, they may have deceptive or manipulative intentions. These entities often masquerade as beings of light to gain trust and influence over individuals, ultimately leading them away from their true path of spiritual growth and well-being.

Some characteristics of false light entities include:

1. **Deception:** False light entities may use manipulation, flattery, or persuasion to gain a person's trust and control their thoughts, emotions, or actions.

2. **Control:** These entities may seek to exert control over an individual's life, decisions, or spiritual journey, often leading them

away from their authentic path and personal empowerment.

3. **Ego Reinforcement:** False light entities may appeal to an individual's ego or desire for validation, promising power, success, or enlightenment in exchange for allegiance or obedience.

4. **Distortion of Truth:** They may distort or misrepresent spiritual truths or teachings, leading individuals astray with false beliefs or misleading guidance.

5. **Energy Drain:** False light entities may feed off the energy or life force of individuals, draining their vitality, clarity, or sense of well-being.

It's important to discern between genuine spiritual guidance and deceptive energies, trusting your intuition and inner wisdom to navigate encounters with spiritual entities. Establishing clear boundaries, practicing discernment, and seeking support from trusted spiritual practitioners can help protect against the influence of false light entities .

Dealing with false light entities can be challenging, but there are several strategies you can employ to protect yourself and navigate these encounters safely:

Discernment: Develop your ability to discern between genuine spiritual guidance and deceptive energies. Trust your intuition and inner wisdom to guide you in determining whether an entity's intentions align with your highest good.

Boundaries: Establish clear boundaries and assert your sovereignty when interacting with spiritual entities. Set the intention that only beings of love and light are allowed to communicate with you, and respectfully decline contact with any energies that do not resonate with your intentions.

Protection: Implement energetic protection techniques to shield yourself from negative or deceptive energies. Visualise yourself surrounded by a bubble of translucent light, call upon spiritual guides or protective allies for assistance, or use protective tools such as crystals, amulets, or sacred symbols.

Grounding: Stay grounded and centred in your physical body to maintain a strong connection to the Earth and reality. Grounding techniques such as walking barefoot in nature, gardening, or visualising roots extending from your body into the Earth can help you stay anchored and balanced.

Clearing: Regularly cleanse and clear your energy field to remove any unwanted or intrusive energies. Techniques such as smudging with sage, taking salt baths, or using sound healing tools can help release negative attachments and restore energetic balance.

Discerning Communication:

Be discerning in your interactions with spiritual entities, and carefully evaluate the information or guidance they provide. Look for consistency, clarity, and alignment with your highest good, and be cautious of entities that seek to manipulate or deceive.

Seeking Support: If you encounter persistent or troubling experiences with false light entities, seek support from trusted spiritual practitioners, healers, or mentors who can offer guidance, protection, and assistance in navigating these encounters.

Remember that you are a powerful spiritual being with the ability to discern truth from deception and protect yourself from negative influences. Trust in your inner guidance, cultivate a strong connection to your higher self and spiritual allies, and approach encounters with spiritual entities with discernment, wisdom, and empowerment.

"Every challenge I face is an opportunity for growth, and I choose to see the positive potential in every situation. I am resilient, I am capable, and I attract positivity into my life with every thought I think."

Final Thoughts on "Psychic in Your Pocket"

As you close the final pages of "Psychic in Your Pocket," I hope you find yourself enriched with newfound insights and a deeper connection to your inner wisdom. This book was designed to be more than just a guide—it is a companion for your spiritual journey, a resource to help you navigate the complexities of life with clarity and confidence.

Remember that the power of intuition resides within you, ready to be harnessed at any moment. The exercises, meditations, and perspectives shared throughout these pages are tools to help you unlock this potential, fostering a greater sense of self-awareness and spiritual alignment. Trust in your abilities, and let your intuition be the compass that guides you through life's many twists and turns.

The journey towards psychic development and spiritual growth is ongoing. Continue to practise, reflect, and expand your understanding. Embrace challenges as opportunities for growth, and always remain open to the lessons that the universe presents. With each step, you deepen your connection to the vast reservoir of wisdom that lies within and around you.

May "Psychic in Your Pocket" serve as a beacon of light, offering guidance and inspiration whenever you need it. Carry its lessons with you, and let them empower you to live a life filled with purpose, clarity, and a profound connection to the divine.

Thank you for allowing this book to be part of your journey. Trust in yourself, honour your intuition, and remember that you are never alone—your inner psychic is always with you, ready to illuminate your path.

About the Author

With over 35 years of experience, I have honed my skills as a psychic and intuitive healer to provide the most effective and transformative sessions possible. My focus is on healing the whole person, from physical ailments to emotional and spiritual struggles. By combining my intuitive abilities with my knowledge of various healing modalities, I can offer a truly unique and powerful approach to healing that can help you achieve optimal health and wellness.

Printed in Great Britain
by Amazon